THE ONE-MINUTE GRATITUDE JOURNAL

This Journal belongs to

_____

ISBN-10: 1523242701
ISBN-13: 978-1523242702

Gratitude

Gratitude is a feeling of appreciation for what one has. It is a feeling of thankfulness for the blessings we have received. Cultivating an attitude of gratitude yields many benefits: physical, mental and spiritual. Feeling gratitude in the present moment makes you happier and more relaxed, and improves your overall health and well-being.

Gratitude is the fairest blossom which springs from the soul.
~ Henry Ward Beecher

Gratitude doesn't just have to be about the big things. It can also be for small, everyday events. You can be thankful for simple things such as enjoying a movie or just talking to an old friend for the first time in a long while. There is always something that you can be grateful for in your life. It is all about appreciating the things around you rather than taking them all for granted.

Write down three to five things that you are grateful for each day. You will not only feel good as you write them down, but you will experience gratitude during the day as well. A person experiencing gratitude feels a sense of joy and abundance in their life. They also feel more connected with other people and have increased energy.

Gratitude should always be expressed in the present tense and is more powerful when combined with the perceived benefit so that an emotional connection is made. Instead of writing, *"I am grateful for my health and well-being,"* it is better to write, *"I am grateful for my health and well-being and it makes me feel great."*

> *No duty is more urgent than that of returning thanks.*
> ~ James Allen

One of the healthiest and most positive things we can do in our lives is to express our gratitude to the people around us. Tell someone how much you appreciate them. Tell someone that something they did mattered to you. When people make an impact, let them know. We are usually too quick to point out people's faults and ways in which they have wronged us, while slow to bestow recognition for good deeds and favors.

If someone makes you feel good, make them feel good too. By expressing our gratitude to others, we are making the world a better place and encouraging the things that we want to see more of. Say, *"Thank you."* Make a difference. Seek out the best in people and when you find it, say something about it.

> *Find ecstasy in life; the mere sense of living is joy enough.*
> ~ Emily Dickinson

There are pages in this journal where you can just draw something. If you don't feel like drawing anything, simply paste a beautiful picture onto this page. Our minds react better to imagery and this is a great way to feel gratitude and appreciation.

Gratitude makes us more optimistic and compassionate. True happiness lies within us. By keeping a record of your gratitude in a journal, you will store positive energy, gain clarity in your life, and have greater control of your thoughts and emotions.

Each day, write down three to five things that you are grateful for in this journal and turn your ordinary moments into blessings.

Day: _Thurs_ Date: 6 / 1 / 17

Today I am *Grateful* for (1) Having three good photos taken: DMV, Passport, + Uber Optics; (2) Meeting Molly (make-up artist / ~~soft shell~~) + Nancy (photographer + owner @ Uber), and (3) Finding a silk scarf in beautiful blues + greens at Red Umbrella Consignmt. Shop.

Let us be grateful to people who make us happy, they are the charming gardeners who make our souls blossom. ~ *Marcel Proust*

Day: _Fri_ Date: 6 / 2 / 17

Today I am *Grateful* for (1) Enjoyed laughing + joking with Hilda while she cleaned my house; (2) With her help, made a bean salad with corn + edamame that turned out well; and (3) Enjoyed trying relaxing teas like Celestial's "Tension Tamer" + Traditional Medicinal's "Nighty Night."

Day: Sat   Date: 6 / 3 / 17

Today I am *Grateful* for (1) Finding for Toby a small crate + dog travel "suitcase" at the Lily's Legacy rummage sale; (2) Choosing a lovely new pair of glasses at Uber; and (3) seeing the positive response of others to the photo of Jarquin I put on FB for his b'day.

The essence of all beautiful art, all great art, is gratitude. ~ Friedrich Nietzsche

Day: Sun   Date: 6 / 4 / 17

Today I am *Grateful* for (1) Finding + chatting with a new gal to trim my hair, Samantha @ Supercuts; (2) Getting help from friends on FB in finding a restaurant for my 6/11 b'day meal w/ Steve; and (3) Finally making my asymmetrical black rice display dish for beautiful rocks.

Day: _Mon_ Date: 6 / 5 / 17

Today I am *Grateful* for (1) Enjoying my first in-depth book about "positive psychology," Seligman's "Authentic Happiness"; (2) Getting all bills paid before my departure; (3) Being able to renew PCS life ins. for Steve, taking good care of him.

The thankful receiver bears a plentiful harvest. ~ *William Blake*

Day: _Tues._ Date: 6 / 6 / 17

Today I am *Grateful* for (1) Going to Essex to see Jenny for my 64th birthday! (2) Making a flight-saving connection in Chicago, only because my wheelchair driver ran! (3) Having Jenny pick me up at the airport, seeing Jerry again, + having a bathroom to myself.

Day: **Wed.** Date: 6 / 7 / 17

Today I am *Grateful* for (1) Exploring the local grocery store together, J introducing me to diet items (like Halo Top) & me introducing teas (like Tension Tamer); (2) J's great salmon filets for dinner; (3) antique + seashell shopping in Essex; (4) ~~Lobster salad~~ ~~at Dog Watch~~

There is only one way to happiness and that is to cease worrying about things which are beyond the power of our will. ~ *Epictetus*

Day: **Thurs.** Date: 6 / 8 / 17

Today I am *Grateful* for (1) Visiting nearby Stonington, meeting Marc the jewelry at Black Orchid + having ~~lobster~~ lobster salad at the Dog Watch; (2) Finding a printer's work box display at a garage sale; and (3) talking over old times, like her ~~watching~~ seeing the removal of my father's body from #8 Chico Court.

Day: Fri, 6/9   Date: 6/9/2017

Today I am *Grateful* for (1) A lovely visit w/ Cordelia + Jake + Addie, mostly reviewing our mutual interests in Ancestry.com; (2) Hearing Gerry review his hearing loss from age 14 + getting new aids; (3) Scoring some great photos!

Be sure you put your feet in the right place, then stand firm.
~ *Abraham Lincoln*

Day: Sat   Date: June 10

Today I am *Grateful* for (1) Regardless of the #, I am delighted to have another b'day, in good health + all caught up with my lifestyle "shoulds" (like drs? apptr. CDL renewal, new glasses, etc.) + at my prime. (2) feeling closer to Jenny than I dared hope for, and (3) Steamed clams + a HUGE lobster for dinner! Also The Newport Mansions

Day: _Sun_   Date: 6/11/17

Today I am *Grateful* for (1) Having Steve pick me up at SFO; (2) Going home to poodle!, and (3) having goodies in the mail to unwrap + in my suitcase to pull out + organize. And then, (4) getting to sleep off my ~jetty~ jetlag and too few hours of sleep in CT.

Positive anything is better than negative nothing. ~ Elbert Hubbard

Day: _Mon_   Date: 6/12/17

Today I am *Grateful* for (1) Glad to be back at Tai Chi, collecting my latest three embossed T-shirts; (2) Shopping at Whole Foods to restock our empty pantry with some of my favorites; and (3) Back to spending time with Poodle and sleeping and unpacking, happy to be getting back to "normal." A nice day off!

Day: Tues.   Date: 6 / 13 / 17

Her last day in CA.

Today I am *Grateful* for (1) Lunch w/
Andi at Guaymas Restaurant
in ~~Bl~~ Belvedere. (2) She
drove + treated me to lunch
for my b'day, both much
appreciated. (3) And absolutely
perfect weather, lovely to eat
out on the patio by the Bay!

The direction of the mind is more important than its progress. ~ *Joseph Joubert*

Day: Wed   Date: 6 / 14 / 17

Today I am *Grateful* for (1) Had a
pedicure w/ Hann today,
~~adhell~~ and she does me personally
now ~~because~~ of my nail fungus.
What a ~~thorough~~ job she does!
(2) My Tai Chi class - will miss
it while I'm gone; and (3) Flag
Day - a hope/beacon of America
in these dark days of Trump.

Day: Thurs   Date: 6 / 15 / 17

Today I am *Grateful* for (1) having a repeat Pap smear—too few cells the first time—and my final Hep B shot. So that wraps up all my routine drs' visits for now, w/ EVERYTHING done! (2) having Lizbuck treat me and Steve to dinner at ~~Bubble~~ Cucina Paradiso; and (3) my manicure w/ Diana.

Happiness is not an ideal of reason, but of imagination. ~ *Immanuel Kant*

Day: Fri   Date: 6 / 16 / 17

Today I am *Grateful* for (1) Hilda + her crew! I love a clean house + am grateful to have her assistance w/ special projects. (2) My souvenirs from CT—esp. my little bronze frog. (3) My vast selection of hot teas — these days a part of my daily routine, enjoyed around the clock.

Day: Sat   Date: 6 / 17 / 17

Today I am *Grateful* for (1) A chance
to play w/ my shell collec-
tion today - so soothing. (2)
My Thai lunches, especially
w/ coconut water - healthy + low
cal. (3) ~~illegible~~
~~illegible~~
~~illegible~~ New Nordstrom pants -

Courtesies of a small and trivial character are the ones which strike deepest in
the grateful and appreciating heart. ~ *Henry Clay*

Day: Sun   Date: 6 / 18 / 17

Today I am *Grateful* for (1) Father's Day,
even tho' Ryan + Steve are
estranged. (2) Dinner at Volpi's,
Steve's treat. (3) Excellent
~~illegible~~ cioppino (for me) +
steamed clams (for him). (3)
A nice chance for Fish + I to
reconnect before I leave +
a chance for him to do a
little self-soothing in what I know
is a difficult week for him.

14

Day: ~~Monday~~ Date: 6 / 19 / 17

Despite change of planes in Chicago.

Today I am *Grateful* for (1) Leaving for Cuba, as far as Miami! (2) No problems from SFO → MIA. ~~met my travel scholars group at the Miami airport~~ ~~they took discrete~~ ~~go groups.~~ (3) Cambria Suites Blue Lagoon Hotel — nicely appointed. Modern & comfortable.

The art of being happy lies in the power of extracting happiness from common things. ~ *Henry Ward Beecher*

Day: Tues Date: 6 / ~~19~~ 20 / 17

Got my Cuban visa today.

Today I am *Grateful* for (1) Leaving for Cuba! ~~my Cuban visa~~. (2) ~~met my travel group~~ ~~Before~~ Before I forget, the latest Shalyndria screw-up: she forgot to check her credit status at Oregon State so missed out on ~~the~~ both her graduation + her commissioning into the USAF. In any case, we weren't invited. Glad not to have to fake "happy family" again. ~~she boycotted in support of us.~~

Day: Wed   Date: 6 /21 /17

last night.

Today I am *Grateful* for (1) My travel group from Road Scholar, which I met. Seems like a good bunch + Alex Vicente is a good guide. (2) Left miami for Cienfuegos. Martha, the feisty black gal, was my seatmate on the flight. We bonded. (3) Met Hector, our guide, + ate in a Persian castle, meant to be a casino.

Happiness resides not in possessions, and not in gold, happiness dwells in the soul. ~ *Democritus*

Day: Thurs   Date: 6/22 / 16

Today I am *Grateful* for (1) A good hotel + a comfy room. Excellent breakfast buffet. (2) Today's tour of the city of Cienfuegos: Saw "octomom" statue, amazing carver who LAZARO sculpts Cuba's country folk out of abandoned wood, ceramic shop w/ its workers, and (3) really enjoyed a Cienfuegos youth Chamber orchestra — loved their music + bought their CD.

16

Day: Fri   Date: 6 /23/ 17

Today I am *Grateful* for (1) Visiting three
food markets - ration store,
sm. general grocery, + a Farmers'
Mkt. - So grateful to have the food
we do back home. (2) Went to a
seniors' center where we learned
about ~~about~~ the "danzón," a slow dance,
and the secret language of fans. (3)
Also, the Che Guevara memorial, a
kids dance performance,

Wonder is the desire for knowledge. ~ *Thomas Aquinas*

Day: Sat   Date: ~~Sat~~ 6/24/17

Today I am *Grateful* for ~~Sat~~ (1) Saw rice
~~hay~~ being dried on the highway
~~E~~ along with a tour of the Santa
Clara war museum. (2) Had
lunch at Playa Girón, site of the
Bay of Pigs invasion, and also
Hemingway's "Finca Virgia" home &
his boat "Pilar." Then onto the
historic "Hotel Nacional de Cuba." (3)
Larry's 64th bday. I miss having a
best friend, but I don't miss him.

Day: Sun   Date: 6 / 25 / 17

Today I am *Grateful* for (1) ~~an interesting history lecture on US/Cuban relations~~ (2) "Carnival" ladies in the park, (3) the cigar-rolling lady at the hotel, (4) Hemingway's watering holes—like La Bodequita + La Bar del Medio + Ambos Mundos, and (5) seeing streets paved with ironwood instead of cobblestones.

Things do not change; we change. ~ Henry David Thoreau

Cigar Night! ⌐

Day: Mon   Date: 6 / 26 / 17

Today I am *Grateful* for ⌐ #1 above, the lecture, belongs here, (2) our visit to the Christopher Columbus Cemetary & (2) my retrieval from same, after the bus left w/o me, (3) the "Havana Queens" dance party performance, (4) the Che Guevara bldg., and (5) Our chance to chat w/ Maria (22) & about how young Cubans see their country, and a silly dinner w/ RAQUEL, DONNA, + HAZEL.

Day: Tues   Date: 6/27/17

Today I am *Grateful* for (1) a lecture on religion + religiousity in Cuba, (2) a tour of Havana's fine arts museum, and (3) the night of the classic cars! They used them to get us to our farewell dinner, where I was asked to present to our three guides — a statement of thanks and the envelopes bearing their tips. (Also, a ladies' choir sang to us.)

Our greatest glory is not in never falling, but in rising every time we fall.
~ Confucius

Day: Wed   Date: 6/28/17

Today I am *Grateful* for (1) An early morning flt. back to Miami from Havana. There were no official goodbyes due to our 4:30 wake-up + 5:30 on-the-bus obligations. Despite some wait time at the Havana airport, we were no longer invested in the group. (2) Raquel — aka Scout — gave me her last Cuban pesos [19] + I bought a Tee for Steve ("Cuban Rebelde"), and (3) I sat w/ Cookie on the shuttle to Cambria.

Draw something

Day: _Thurs_   Date: 6 /29/ ___

Today I am *Grateful* for (1) being on the plane going home. I'm glad I "did" Cuba, but also glad to be returning to my comfort zone. (2)

_____

_____

A single grateful thought toward heaven is the most perfect prayer.
~ *Gotthold Ephraim Lessing*

Day: _Fri_   Date: 6 /30/ 17

Today I am *Grateful* for (1) June is ending. It has always been "my month," and this was an especially good one. But I now enjoy ALL the months + it's time to move on.

_____

_____

21

Day: _____ *Date:* 7/ ___ / ___

Today I am *Grateful* for <u>Important, Kind,</u>
<u>& Useful?</u>

Gratitude is not only the greatest of virtues, but the parent of all the others.
~ *Marcus Tullius Cicero*

Day: _____ *Date:* ___ / ___ / ___

Today I am *Grateful* for _____

Day: .... *Date:* .... / .... /

Today I am *Grateful* for ....

....

....

....

....

....

The pleasure which we most rarely experience gives us greatest delight.
-- *Epictetus*

Day: .... *Date:* .... / .... /

Today I am *Grateful* for ....

....

....

....

....

....

Day: _____ *Date:* ____ / ____ / ____

Today I am *Grateful* for _____

_____

_____

_____

_____

_____

Gratitude is the sign of noble souls. ~ *Aesop Fables*

Day: _____ *Date:* ____ / ____ / ____

Today I am *Grateful* for _____

_____

_____

_____

_____

_____

Day: .... *Date:* ..../ ..../ ....

Today I am *Grateful* for ....

....

....

....

....

....

If a little dreaming is dangerous, the cure for it is not to dream less but to dream more, to dream all the time. ~ *Marcel Proust*

Day: .... *Date:* ..../ ..../ ....

Today I am *Grateful* for ....

....

....

....

....

....

Day: _____ *Date:* ____ / ____ / ____

Today I am *Grateful* for _____

_____

_____

_____

_____

_____

_____

Gratitude is a duty which ought to be paid, but which none have
a right to expect. ~ *Jean-Jacques Rousseau*

Day: _____ *Date:* ____ / ____ / ____

Today I am *Grateful* for _____

_____

_____

_____

_____

_____

Day: _____ *Date:* _____ / _____ / _____

Today I am *Grateful* for _____

_____

_____

_____

_____

_____

Appreciation is a wonderful thing: It makes what is excellent in others
belong to us as well. ~ *Voltaire*

Day: _____ *Date:* _____ / _____ / _____

Today I am *Grateful* for _____

_____

_____

_____

_____

Day: _____ *Date:* ____/ ____/ ____

Today I am *Grateful* for _____

_____

_____

_____

_____

_____

The clearest way into the Universe is through a forest wilderness.
~ *John Muir*

Day: _____ *Date:* ____/ ____/ ____

Today I am *Grateful* for _____

_____

_____

_____

_____

_____

Day: .... *Date:* ....../ ....../ ......

Today I am *Grateful* for ....

....

....

....

....

....

When unhappy, one doubts everything; when happy, one doubts nothing.
~ *Joseph Roux*

Day: .... *Date:* ....../ ....../ ......

Today I am *Grateful* for ....

....

....

....

....

....

Day: _____ *Date:* ____ / ____ / ____

Today I am *Grateful* for _____

_____

_____

_____

_____

_____

Our happiness depends on wisdom all the way. ~ *Sophocles*

Day: _____ *Date:* ____ / ____ / ____

Today I am *Grateful* for _____

_____

_____

_____

_____

_____

Day: .... *Date:* ..... / ..... / .....

Today I am *Grateful* for ....

....

....

....

....

....

....

The most certain sign of wisdom is cheerfulness. ~ *Michel de Montaigne*

Day: .... *Date:* ..... / ..... / .....

Today I am *Grateful* for ....

....

....

....

....

....

Day: _____ *Date:* ____/____/____

Today I am *Grateful* for _____

_____

_____

_____

_____

_____

Believe you can and you're halfway there.
~ *Theodore Roosevelt*

Day: _____ *Date:* ____/____/____

Today I am *Grateful* for _____

_____

_____

_____

_____

_____

Day: .... *Date:* ..../ ..../ ....

Today I am *Grateful* for ....

....

....

....

....

....

Events will take their course, it is no good of being angry at them; he is
happiest who wisely turns them to the best account. ~ *Euripides*

Day: .... *Date:* ..../ ..../ ....

Today I am *Grateful* for ....

....

....

....

....

....

Day: _____ *Date:* ____/____/____

Today I am *Grateful* for _____

_____

_____

_____

_____

_____

Everything has beauty, but not everyone sees it. ~ *Confucius*

Day: _____ *Date:* ____/____/____

Today I am *Grateful* for _____

_____

_____

_____

_____

_____

Draw something

Day: _____ *Date:* _____ / _____ / _____

Today I am *Grateful* for _____

_____

_____

_____

_____

_____

Make it your habit not to be critical about small things.
~ *Edward Everett Hale*

Day: _____ *Date:* _____ / _____ / _____

Today I am *Grateful* for _____

_____

_____

_____

_____

_____

Day: .... *Date:* ...... / ...... / ......

Today I am *Grateful* for ....

....

....

....

....

....

Believe that life is worth living and your belief will help create the fact.
~ *William James*

Day: .... *Date:* ...... / ...... / ......

Today I am *Grateful* for ....

....

....

....

....

....

Day: _____ *Date:* ____/____/____

Today I am *Grateful* for _____

_____

_____

_____

_____

_____

A contented mind is the greatest blessing a man can enjoy in this world.
~ *Joseph Addison*

Day: _____ *Date:* ____/____/____

Today I am *Grateful* for _____

_____

_____

_____

_____

Day: _____ *Date:* _____ / _____ / _____

Today I am *Grateful* for _____

_____

_____

_____

_____

_____

Good actions give strength to ourselves and inspire good actions in others.
~ *Plato*

Day: _____ *Date:* _____ / _____ / _____

Today I am *Grateful* for _____

_____

_____

_____

_____

_____

Day: _____ *Date:* ____/ ____/ _____

Today I am *Grateful* for _____

_____

_____

_____

_____

_____

Our best successes often come after our greatest disappointments.
~ *Henry Ward Beecher*

Day: _____ *Date:* ____/ ____/ _____

Today I am *Grateful* for _____

_____

_____

_____

_____

_____

Day: _____ *Date:* ____ / ____ / ____

Today I am *Grateful* for _____

_____

_____

_____

_____

_____

A loving heart is the beginning of all knowledge. ~ *Thomas Carlyle*

Day: _____ *Date:* ____ / ____ / ____

Today I am *Grateful* for _____

_____

_____

_____

_____

_____

Day: _____ *Date:* ____/ ____/ ____

Today I am *Grateful* for _____

_____

_____

_____

_____

_____

Honesty is the first chapter in the book of wisdom. ~ *Thomas Jefferson*

Day: _____ *Date:* ____/ ____/ ____

Today I am *Grateful* for _____

_____

_____

_____

_____

_____

Day: .... *Date:* .... / .... / ....

Today I am *Grateful* for ....

....

....

....

....

....

Life in abundance comes only through great love.
~ *Elbert Hubbard*

Day: .... *Date:* .... / .... / ....

Today I am *Grateful* for ....

....

....

....

....

....

Day: _____ *Date:* ____ / ____ / ____

Today I am *Grateful* for _____

_____

_____

_____

_____

_____

To live is so startling it leaves little time for anything else. ~ *Emily Dickinson*

Day: _____ *Date:* ____ / ____ / ____

Today I am *Grateful* for _____

_____

_____

_____

_____

_____

Day: .... *Date:* ....../....../......

Today I am *Grateful* for ....

....

....

....

....

....

The way to know life is to love many things. ~ *Vincent Van Gogh*

Day: .... *Date:* ....../....../......

Today I am *Grateful* for ....

....

....

....

....

....

Day: _____ *Date:* ____ / ____ / ____

Today I am *Grateful* for _____

_____

_____

_____

_____

_____

It takes less time to do a thing right, than it does to explain
why you did it wrong. ~ *Henry Wadsworth Longfellow*

Day: _____ *Date:* ____ / ____ / ____

Today I am *Grateful* for _____

_____

_____

_____

_____

_____

Day: .... *Date:* .... / .... / ....

Today I am *Grateful* for ....

....

....

....

....

....

Keep love in your heart. A life without it is like a sunless garden when the
flowers are dead. ~ *Oscar Wilde*

Day: .... *Date:* .... / .... / ....

Today I am *Grateful* for ....

....

....

....

....

....

Day: _____ *Date:* ____ / ____ / ____

Today I am *Grateful* for _____

_____

_____

_____

_____

_____

The future is purchased by the present. ~ *Samuel Johnson*

Day: _____ *Date:* ____ / ____ / ____

Today I am *Grateful* for _____

_____

_____

_____

_____

_____

Day: _____ *Date:* ___/___/___

Today I am *Grateful* for _____

_____

_____

_____

_____

_____

Never do a wrong thing to make a friend or to keep one. ~ *Robert E. Lee*

Day: _____ *Date:* ___/___/___

Today I am *Grateful* for _____

_____

_____

_____

_____

_____

Draw something

Day: .... *Date:* ...... / ...... / ......

Today I am *Grateful* for ....

....

....

....

....

....

Life consists not in holding good cards but in playing those you hold well.
~ *Josh Billings*

Day: .... *Date:* ...... / ...... / ......

Today I am *Grateful* for ....

....

....

....

....

....

Day: _____ *Date:* ____/ ____/ _____

Today I am *Grateful* for _____

_____

_____

_____

_____

_____

Nothing is a waste of time if you use the experience wisely.
~ *Auguste Rodin*

Day: _____ *Date:* ____/ ____/ _____

Today I am *Grateful* for _____

_____

_____

_____

_____

Day: .... *Date:* ..../........../..........

Today I am *Grateful* for ....

....

....

....

....

....

He who knows best knows how little he knows. ~ *Thomas Jefferson*

Day: .... *Date:* ..../........../..........

Today I am *Grateful* for ....

....

....

....

....

....

Day: _____ *Date:* ____ / ____ / ____

Today I am *Grateful* for _____

_____

_____

_____

_____

_____

Great thoughts speak only to the thoughtful mind, but great actions
speak to all mankind. ~ *Theodore Roosevelt*

Day: _____ *Date:* ____ / ____ / ____

Today I am *Grateful* for _____

_____

_____

_____

_____

_____

Day: .... *Date:* .... / .... / ....

Today I am *Grateful* for ....

....

....

....

....

....

Never give up, for that is just the place and time that the tide will turn.
~ *Harriet Beecher Stowe*

Day: .... *Date:* .... / .... / ....

Today I am *Grateful* for ....

....

....

....

....

....

Day: _____ *Date:* ____ / ____ / ____

Today I am *Grateful* for _____

_____

_____

_____

_____

_____

Either I will find a way, or I will make one. ~ *Philip Sidney*

Day: _____ *Date:* ____ / ____ / ____

Today I am *Grateful* for _____

_____

_____

_____

_____

_____

Day: .... *Date:* .... / .... / ....

Today I am *Grateful* for ....

....

....

....

....

....

Do not fear mistakes. You will know failure. Continue to reach out.
~ Benjamin Franklin

Day: .... *Date:* .... / .... / ....

Today I am *Grateful* for ....

....

....

....

....

....

Day: _____ *Date:* ____ / ____ / ____

Today I am *Grateful* for _____

_____

_____

_____

_____

_____

It is costly wisdom that is bought by experience. ~ *Roger Ascham*

Day: _____ *Date:* ____ / ____ / ____

Today I am *Grateful* for _____

_____

_____

_____

_____

_____

Day: _____ *Date:* ____/____/____

Today I am *Grateful* for _____

_____

_____

_____

_____

_____

To love oneself is the beginning of a lifelong romance. ~ *Oscar Wilde*

Day: _____ *Date:* ____/____/____

Today I am *Grateful* for _____

_____

_____

_____

_____

_____

Day: _____ *Date:* ____/____/____

Today I am *Grateful* for _____

_____

_____

_____

_____

_____

Reasoning draws a conclusion, but does not make the conclusion certain,
unless the mind discovers it by the path of experience. ~ *Roger Bacon*

Day: _____ *Date:* ____/____/____

Today I am *Grateful* for _____

_____

_____

_____

_____

_____

Day: _____ *Date:* _____ / _____ / _____

Today I am *Grateful* for _____

_____

_____

_____

_____

_____

Remember when life's path is steep to keep your mind even. ~ *Horace*

Day: _____ *Date.* _____ / _____ / _____

Today I am *Grateful* for _____

_____

_____

_____

_____

_____

Day: _____ *Date:* ____/ ____/ ____

Today I am *Grateful* for _____

_____

_____

_____

_____

_____

Ask me not what I have, but what I am. ~ *Heinrich Heine*

Day: _____ *Date:* ____/ ____/ ____

Today I am *Grateful* for _____

_____

_____

_____

_____

_____

Day: _____ *Date:* _____/_____/_____

Today I am *Grateful* for

_____

_____

_____

_____

_____

_____

The best preparation for tomorrow is to do today's work superbly well.
~ *William Osler*

Day: _____ *Date:* _____/_____/_____

Today I am *Grateful* for

_____

_____

_____

_____

_____

Day: _____ *Date:* ____/ ____/ ____

Today I am *Grateful* for _____

_____

_____

_____

_____

_____

Love always brings difficulties, that is true, but the good side of
it is that it gives energy. ~ *Vincent Van Gogh*

Day: _____ *Date:* ____/ ____/ ____

Today I am *Grateful* for _____

_____

_____

_____

_____

_____

Draw something

Day: _____ *Date:* ____/____/____

Today I am *Grateful* for _____

_____

_____

_____

_____

_____

Little minds are interested in the extraordinary; great minds in the commonplace. ~ *Elbert Hubbard*

Day: _____ *Date:* ____/____/____

Today I am *Grateful* for _____

_____

_____

_____

_____

_____

Day: _____ *Date:* ____/____/____

Today I am *Grateful* for _____

_____
_____
_____
_____
_____

When you're finished changing, you're finished. ~ *Benjamin Franklin*

Day: _____ *Date.* ____/____/____

Today I am *Grateful* for _____

_____
_____
_____
_____
_____

Day: _____ *Date:* ____ / ____ / ____

Today I am *Grateful* for _____

_____

_____

_____

_____

_____

Do not mind anything that anyone tells you about anyone else. Judge everyone
and everything for yourself. ~ *Henry James*

Day: _____ *Date:* ____ / ____ / ____

Today I am *Grateful* for _____

_____

_____

_____

_____

_____

Day: .... *Date:* .... / .... / ....

Today I am *Grateful* for ....

_____

_____

_____

_____

_____

It is our attitude at the beginning of a difficult task which, more than
anything else, will affect its successful outcome. ~ *William James*

Day. .... *Date:* .... / .... / ....

Today I am *Grateful* for ....

_____

_____

_____

_____

_____

Day: _____ *Date:* ____/ ____/ _____

Today I am *Grateful* for _____

_____

_____

_____

_____

_____

Cheerfulness is the best promoter of health and is as friendly to the
mind as to the body. ~ *Joseph Addison*

Day: _____ *Date:* ____/ ____/ _____

Today I am *Grateful* for _____

_____

_____

_____

_____

_____

Day: _____ *Date:* ____/____/____

Today I am *Grateful* for _____

_____

_____

_____

_____

_____

I dwell in possibility. ~ *Emily Dickinson*

Day: _____ *Date:* ____/____/____

Today I am *Grateful* for _____

_____

_____

_____

_____

_____

Day: _____ *Date:* ____/ ____/ ____

Today I am *Grateful* for _____

_____

_____

_____

_____

_____

Creativity is not the finding of a thing, but the making something out of it
after it is found. ~ *James Russell Lowell*

Day: _____ *Date:* ____/ ____/ ____

Today I am *Grateful* for _____

_____

_____

_____

_____

_____

Day: _____ *Date:* ____/____/____

Today I am *Grateful* for _____

_____

_____

_____

_____

_____

A thing of beauty is a joy forever: its loveliness increases; it will never pass
into nothingness. ~ *John Keats*

Day: _____ *Date:* ____/____/____

Today I am *Grateful* for _____

_____

_____

_____

_____

_____

Day: _____ *Date:* ____/____/____

Today I am *Grateful* for _____

_____

_____

_____

_____

_____

To have courage for whatever comes in life - everything lies in that.
~ *Saint Teresa of Avila*

Day: _____ *Date:* ____/____/____

Today I am *Grateful* for _____

_____

_____

_____

_____

_____

Day: _____ *Date:* _____/_____/_____

Today I am *Grateful* for _____

_____

_____

_____

_____

_____

We build too many walls and not enough bridges. ~ *Isaac Newton*

Day: _____ *Date:* _____/_____/_____

Today I am *Grateful* for _____

_____

_____

_____

_____

_____

Day: _____ *Date:* ____ / ____ / ____

Today I am *Grateful* for _____

_____

_____

_____

_____

_____

After a storm comes a calm. ~ *Matthew Henry*

Day: _____ *Date:* ____ / ____ / ____

Today I am *Grateful* for _____

_____

_____

_____

_____

Day: _____ *Date:* _____ / _____ / _____

Today I am *Grateful* for _____

_____

_____

_____

_____

_____

A thousand words will not leave so deep an impression as one deed.
~ *Henrik Ibsen*

Day: _____ *Date:* _____ / _____ / _____

Today I am *Grateful* for _____

_____

_____

_____

_____

Day: _____ *Date:* ____ / ____ / ____

Today I am *Grateful* for _____

_____

_____

_____

_____

_____

All experience is an arch, to build upon. ~ *Henry Adams*

Day: _____ *Date:* ____ / ____ / ____

Today I am *Grateful* for _____

_____

_____

_____

_____

_____

Day: .... *Date:* .... / .... / ....

Today I am *Grateful* for ....

Thank God every morning when you get up that you have something to do
that day, which must be done, whether you like it or not. ~ *James Russell Lowell*

Day: .... *Date:* .... / .... / ....

Today I am *Grateful* for ....

Draw something

Day: .... *Date:* ..../......../........

Today I am *Grateful* for ....

....

....

....

....

....

Genius is the ability to renew one's emotions in daily experience.
~ *Paul Cezanne*

Day: .... *Date:* ..../......../........

Today I am *Grateful* for ....

....

....

....

....

....

Day: _____ *Date:* ____/____/____

Today I am *Grateful* for _____

_____

_____

_____

_____

How very little can be done under the spirit of fear. ~ *Florence Nightingale*

Day: _____ *Date:* ____/____/____

Today I am *Grateful* for _____

_____

_____

_____

_____

Day: _____ *Date:* ____ / ____ / ____

Today I am *Grateful* for _____

_____

_____

_____

_____

_____

> Doubt comes in at the window when inquiry is denied at the door.
> ~ *Benjamin Jowett*

Day. _____ *Date:* ____ / ____ / ____

Today I am *Grateful* for _____

_____

_____

_____

_____

_____

Day: _____ *Date:* ____/ ____/ ____

Today I am *Grateful* for _____

_____

_____

_____

_____

_____

Life is not a matter of holding good cards, but of playing a poor hand well.
~ *Robert Louis Stevenson*

Day: _____ *Date:* ____/ ____/ ____

Today I am *Grateful* for _____

_____

_____

_____

_____

_____

Day: _____ *Date:* _____ / _____ / _____

Today I am *Grateful* for _____

_____

_____

_____

_____

_____

With an eye made quiet by the power of harmony, and the deep power
of joy, we see into the life of things. ~ *William Wordsworth*

Day: _____ *Date.* _____ / _____ / _____

Today I am *Grateful* for _____

_____

_____

_____

_____

_____

Day: _____ *Date:* ____ / ____ / ____

Today I am *Grateful* for _____

_____

_____

_____

_____

_____

We consume our tomorrows fretting about our yesterdays. ~ *Persius*

Day: _____ *Date:* ____ / ____ / ____

Today I am *Grateful* for _____

_____

_____

_____

_____

_____

Day: _____ *Date:* ____ / ____ / ____

Today I am *Grateful* for _____

_____

_____

_____

_____

_____

A gentle word, a kind look, a good-natured smile can work wonders and accomplish miracles. ~ *William Hazlitt*

Day: _____ *Date:* ____ / ____ / ____

Today I am *Grateful* for _____

_____

_____

_____

_____

_____

Day: _____ *Date:* ____/____/____

Today I am *Grateful* for _____

_____

_____

_____

_____

No man is an island, entire of itself; every man is a piece of the continent.
~ John Donne

Day: _____ *Date:* ____/____/____

Today I am *Grateful* for _____

_____

_____

_____

_____

Day: _____ *Date:* ____/____/____

Today I am *Grateful* for _____

_____

_____

_____

_____

_____

Live your life as though your every act were to become a universal law.
~ *Immanuel Kant*

Day: _____ *Date:* ____/____/____

Today I am *Grateful* for _____

_____

_____

_____

_____

_____

Day: _____ *Date:* ____ / ____ / ____

Today I am *Grateful* for _____

_____

_____

_____

_____

_____

If you want the present to be different from the past, study the past.
~ *Baruch Spinoza*

Day: _____ *Date:* ____ / ____ / ____

Today I am *Grateful* for _____

_____

_____

_____

_____

_____

Day: _____ *Date:* ____/____/____

Today I am *Grateful* for _____

_____

_____

_____

_____

_____

The measure of a man's real character is what he would do if he knew he
would never be found out. ~ *Thomas Babington Macaulay*

Day: _____ *Date:* ____/____/____

Today I am *Grateful* for _____

_____

_____

_____

_____

_____

Day: _____ *Date:* ____ / ____ / ____

Today I am *Grateful* for _____

_____

_____

_____

_____

The mountains are calling and I must go. ~ *John Muir*

Day: _____ *Date:* ____ / ____ / ____

Today I am *Grateful* for _____

_____

_____

_____

_____

Day: _____ Date: ____/____/_____

Today I am *Grateful* for _____

_____

_____

_____

_____

_____

Begin, be bold and venture to be wise. ~ *Horace*

Day: _____ Date: ____/____/_____

Today I am *Grateful* for _____

_____

_____

_____

_____

_____

Day: _____ *Date:* ____ / ____ / ____

Today I am *Grateful* for _____

_____

_____

_____

_____

_____

Of the blessings set before you make your choice, and be content.
~ *Samuel Johnson*

Day: _____ *Date:* ____ / ____ / ____

Today I am *Grateful* for _____

_____

_____

_____

_____

_____

Draw something

Day: _____ *Date:* ____/ ____/ ____

Today I am *Grateful* for _____

_____

_____

_____

_____

_____

Friends are the sunshine of life. ~ *John Hay*

Day: _____ *Date:* ____/ ____/ ____

Today I am *Grateful* for _____

_____

_____

_____

_____

_____

Day: _____ *Date:* _____/_____/_____

Today I am *Grateful* for _____

_____

_____

_____

_____

_____

Let us be of good cheer, however, remembering that the misfortunes
hardest to bear are those which never come. ~ *James Russell Lowell*

Day: _____ *Date:* _____/_____/_____

Today I am *Grateful* for _____

_____

_____

_____

_____

_____

Day: _____ *Date:* ____ / ____ / ____

Today I am *Grateful* for _____

_____

_____

_____

_____

_____

He who knows that enough is enough will always have enough. ~ *Lao Tzu*

Day: _____ *Date:* ____ / ____ / ____

Today I am *Grateful* for _____

_____

_____

_____

_____

_____

Day: _____ *Date:* ___ / ___ / ___

Today I am *Grateful* for _____

_____

_____

_____

_____

_____

You cannot do a kindness too soon, for you never know how soon
it will be too late. ~ *Ralph Waldo Emerson*

Day: _____ *Date:* ___ / ___ / ___

Today I am *Grateful* for _____

_____

_____

_____

_____

Day: _____ *Date:* ____ / ____ / ____

Today I am *Grateful* for _____

_____

_____

_____

_____

_____

Real happiness is cheap enough, yet how dearly we pay for its counterfeit.
~ *Hosea Ballou*

Day: _____ *Date:* ____ / ____ / ____

Today I am *Grateful* for _____

_____

_____

_____

_____

_____

Day: _____ *Date:* ____/____/_____

Today I am *Grateful* for _____

_____

_____

_____

_____

_____

Gratitude is a state of being and should be directed towards everything that
you are creating in this life.

Day: _____ *Date:* ____/____/_____

Today I am *Grateful* for _____

_____

_____

_____

_____

_____

Day: _____ *Date:* ____ / ____ / ____

Today I am *Grateful* for _____

_____

_____

_____

_____

The power of imagination makes us infinite. ~ *John Muir*

Day: _____ *Date:* ____ / ____ / ____

Today I am *Grateful* for _____

_____

_____

_____

_____

Day: _____ *Date:* ___/___/___

Today I am *Grateful* for _____

_____

_____

_____

_____

_____

Happiness is a choice that requires effort at times. ~ *Aeschylus*

Day: _____ *Date:* ___/___/___

Today I am *Grateful* for _____

_____

_____

_____

_____

_____

Day: _____ *Date:* ____/____/____

Today I am *Grateful* for _____

_____

_____

_____

_____

_____

What we obtain too cheap, we esteem too lightly; it is dearness only that gives
everything its value. ~ *Thomas Paine*

Day: _____ *Date:* ____/____/____

Today I am *Grateful* for _____

_____

_____

_____

_____

_____

Day: _____ *Date:* ____ / ____ / ____

Today I am *Grateful* for _____

_____

_____

_____

_____

_____

What worries you, masters you. ~ *John Locke*

Day: _____ *Date:* ____ / ____ / ____

Today I am *Grateful* for _____

_____

_____

_____

_____

Day: _____ *Date:* ____/____/____

Today I am *Grateful* for _____

_____

_____

_____

_____

_____

All things are difficult before they are easy. ~ *Thomas Fuller*

Day: _____ *Date:* ____/____/____

Today I am *Grateful* for _____

_____

_____

_____

_____

_____

Day: _____ *Date:* ____ / ____ / ____

Today I am *Grateful* for _____

_____

_____

_____

_____

_____

Who knows, the mind has the key to all things besides. ~ *Amos Bronson Alcott*

Day: _____ *Date:* ____ / ____ / ____

Today I am *Grateful* for _____

_____

_____

_____

_____

Day: _____ *Date:* ____/____/____

Today I am *Grateful* for _____

_____

_____

_____

_____

_____

The purpose creates the machine. ~ *Arthur Young*

Day: _____ *Date:* ____/____/____

Today I am *Grateful* for _____

_____

_____

_____

_____

_____

Day: .... *Date:* ...... / ...... / ......

Today I am *Grateful* for ....

_____

_____

_____

_____

_____

Knowing is not enough; we must apply. Willing is not enough; we must do.
~ *Johann Wolfgang von Goethe*

Day: .... *Date:* ...... / ...... / ......

Today I am *Grateful* for ....

_____

_____

_____

_____

_____

Draw something

Notes

Notes

Made in the USA
San Bernardino, CA
27 May 2017